W9-AVE-475

Wembley Fraggle Gets the Story

By Deborah Perlberg
Pictures by Steven Schindler

Muppet Press
Holt, Rinehart and Winston
NEW YORK

Copyright © 1984 by Henson Associates, Inc.
Fraggle Rock, Fraggles, Muppets, and character
names are trademarks of Henson Associates, Inc.
All rights reserved, including the right to reproduce this
book or portions thereof in any form.
Published by Holt, Rinehart and Winston,
383 Madison Avenue, New York, New York 10017.

Library of Congress Cataloging in Publication Data
Perlberg, Deborah.
Wembley Fraggle gets the story.
Summary: Wembley and his friends decide to write and
publish the First-Ever Fraggle Rock Newspaper.
[1. Puppets—Fiction. 2. Newspaper publishing—
Fiction. 3. Journalism—Fiction] I. Schindler, S. D., ill.
II. Title.
PZ7.P43235We 1984   [E]   84-6586

ISBN: 0-03-000718-6
First Edition

Printed in the United States of America
1 3 5 7 9 10 8 6 4 2

ISBN 0-03-000718-6

Contents

wem·ble \'wem-bəl\ *vi* **wem·bled; wem·bling** [fr. OF *wemb* circular] **1 :** to travel in circles; to be unable to get anywhere   **2 :** to be indecisive; to not be able to make up one's mind   **3 :** to be overly agree-able; to not take a stand on anything

From *The Dictionary of the Fragglish Language*

Wemble, wemble, skip and hop,
Round and round we go, hey!
Wemblers start and never stop,
Wemblers flip and Wemblers flop,
Round and round we go, hey!
Round and round we go!

From an old Fraggle nursery rhyme

I

The First-Ever Fraggle Rock Newspaper

"Go ahead, Wembley. You choose first."

Wembley Fraggle stared. There was a rainbow in front of him! Actually, it wasn't a real rainbow, although Fraggle Rock has rainbows from time to time. This rainbow was made up of a fistful of brand-new, unused crayons—every color of crayon that Wembley had ever seen. They were beautiful!

"Gee," Wembley said, scratching his fuzzy yellow head. "I don't know which one to pick."

"Come on, little Wembley," said Mokey kindly. "Just take any color. I want to share my new crayons with my four best friends."

"Forget it, Mokey." Red Fraggle shook her head impatiently. "Wembley couldn't decide between white and white. I want *that* one!" And Red grabbed a bright orange crayon that was almost exactly the color of her pigtails.

I

"How about you, Gobo?" asked Mokey. "Which color do you want?"

"I think I'll take the green," Gobo said. "It reminds me of the color of the Mossy Marsh that I explored just the other day. How about you, Boober? What color will you pick?"

Boober Fraggle looked gloomily at the last three crayons. "Crayons," he said with a sigh, "make terrible laundry stains. I think I'll go wash some socks." Laundry was Boober's job in Fraggle Rock, and he loved doing it more than anything.

"Boober, you're such a drag!" Red cried. "Who cares about a dumb thing like laundry when we're all going to play the Tell-a-Story Game?"

"*I* care," muttered Boober as he headed off to his cave.

"I'll take the blue crayon, Wembley," Mokey said. "That leaves yellow and red. Why don't you take the yellow? It's such a cheerful color."

"All right, Mokey," Wembley said happily. "Whatever you say. Although the red is really pretty, too."

Mokey, Red, Gobo, and Wembley were sitting on a ledge in the Great Hall of Fraggle Rock. Fraggle Rock is a very special place, full of caves and pools and Fraggles—thousands of Fraggles. It's a hard place to find because it is underground. But once you are there, you are sure to see all the Fraggles running and swimming and making music and playing games. That's because Fraggles love to have fun more than anything else in the world!

"Hey, let's move it, okay?" Red was getting impatient. "If we don't start playing soon, we'll never finish in time for lunch!"

"All right," Mokey said. "Our story begins with a big pond— bigger than the pond in the Great Hall of Fraggle Rock. It is a peaceful, beautiful, and magical pond." As she spoke, Mokey started to draw. Everyone leaned over to look at the big blue pond that Mokey was drawing.

"No Fraggle had ever seen this pond before," she went on. "Until one day..." She finished drawing and turned to Red.

"One day," Red said, taking the paper and drawing furiously with her orange crayon, "the Bravest Fraggle in the Rock appeared. She ran faster than any Fraggle had ever run before, and jumped higher, and swam better." Red drew some more. The Brave Fraggle was beginning to look a lot like her.

"I—I mean she—ran toward the pond. She jumped so high that she was almost flying, and came down in a perfect double-the-loop dive with a half twist!"

"My turn!" Gobo cried. He picked up his crayon and began to draw some long, tangled green weeds at the bottom of the pond.

"When the Brave Fraggle reached the bottom of the pond, she got caught in these terrible weeds," he said. "It was a really dangerous adventure—almost as dangerous as the adventures I have been in myself."

"Or the ones you *claim* to have been in," Red whispered.

"Anyway," Gobo went on, ignoring her, "the Brave Fraggle tried awfully hard to get free of the weeds, but she couldn't."

"What happened then?" asked Mokey.

"Yeah, what happened?" Red echoed.

"I don't know," said Gobo, shaking his head. Then he turned to Wembley, who was clutching his yellow crayon in excitement. "What happened, Wembley?"

"Uh...she...ah...oh, no! Is it my turn already?" Wembley looked around at his friends in dismay. "I can't decide!"

"Boy, Wembley! You can never decide about *anything*!" Red

shook her head. "You sure know how to mess up a Tell-a-Story Game."

"But it's so hard to choose!" Wembley said miserably. "I don't want to pick the wrong thing, or make anyone mad at me."

"There is no right or wrong thing, Wembley," Gobo said. "It's just a story. It's all made up."

"Oh," Wembley said. "That's different." He sat there for a moment thinking. Then he turned to Gobo.

"What do you think, Gobo?" he asked. "How do you think it should end?"

"Wembley..." Gobo sighed and shook his head. He gently took the yellow crayon away from Wembley. Gobo thought for a moment, and then he started to draw.

"The Brave Fraggle thought her life was over," Gobo said, drawing. "But suddenly the sun, which had been behind a cloud, came out and started to shine. It shone so hard that all the water in the pond dried up—and the Brave Fraggle was saved!" Gobo finished the drawing, and held it up for everyone to see. A big, yellow sun shone over the pond, and the Brave Fraggle was smiling a big yellow smile.

"What a wonderful ending!" Wembley breathed. "Boy, Gobo, I never could have come up with anything half as wonderful as that!"

"It really *is* a nice story," Mokey agreed. "And we all had interesting things to add to it. When we all write together, it's even more fun than when I write in my diary all alone."

"It *is* fun to write together," said Red. "And it does look terrific. Why don't we post it on the Big Rock, where all the Fraggles can see it?" Red pointed to the rock where Fraggle posters and notices were hung.

"Sure, why not?" said Gobo. "Every Fraggle always loves a good story." The others all nodded. It was true: Fraggles loved good stories more than almost anything else.

"Wait!" Red cried. An idea was growing in her head. Her eyes were bright and her red pigtails shook. "I know! Let's play an even bigger Tell-a-Story Game! Let's *all* write stories—lots of stories! Let's write a whole collection of stories, all about Fraggle Rock. And all the other Fraggles can read them!"

"You know, that would be fun!" Mokey jumped in. "It would

be a little like my diary, but from all of us to all of them! And it could have pictures, and writing—what a wonderful idea, Red!"

"Aw, it was nothing," Red shrugged. But secretly she was thrilled.

"Okay, then." Red cleared her throat. "We're all going to play the—the Fraggle Rock Lots of Stories Game! We'll all write for it, and I'll be—I'll be the Chief Story Fraggle!"

"We ought to be able to think up a better name for the game than that," Gobo said.

"Well, I can't do *everything*!" Red said. "I came up with the game, *you* come up with the name."

The four Fraggles looked at one another blankly. Suddenly Gobo jumped up. "I knew this game reminded me of something!" he said mysteriously. "Wait here!" And he headed off in the direction of the cave he shared with Wembley.

He was back in no time, carrying a postcard. "Oh, no," Red muttered. "A postcard from Gobo's Uncle Traveling Matt. Bor ing!"

Gobo's Uncle Traveling Matt was perhaps the bravest Fraggle who had ever lived. He was busy exploring Outer Space at the moment, which is the Fragglish term for our world. He sent postcards back to Gobo describing all the strange and wonderful things he found there. And Gobo *always* read these postcards aloud to whoever was around. Sometimes Red just wasn't in the mood.

"Listen to this," Gobo said. " 'Dear Nephew Gobo: The Silly Creatures here sometimes do the oddest things. Very often, when they're walking around or riding in their strange transportation systems, they carry large sheets of paper in front of their noses. At first I thought they were hiding and didn't want to be recognized. But then I looked at one of these papers. It turns out that the Silly Creatures are actually *reading* them! They're called newspapers, and they have lots of stories and pictures in them. Sometimes the Silly Creatures are not so weird after all. Reading *is* a wonderful thing!' "

Gobo looked up. "We can call it a newspaper, Red!" he cried. "The First-Ever Fraggle Rock Newspaper! Isn't it a great word?"

"It does have a certain ring to it," Red admitted. "Newspaper. I like it. Are we all agreed?"

"Yes!" Mokey and Wembley chimed.

"All right. Newspaper it is. Now, what are we going to put in it?"

"I like the drawing pictures part," said Mokey. "But I want to write something, too."

"I know one thing you'd be great at, Mokey," Gobo replied. "Traveling Matt says here that there's a place in the newspaper where someone gives advice to Silly Creatures in distress. Why don't you have some Fraggles in distress write to you with problems you can solve?"

"Where's Distress?" asked Wembley. "And what are Fraggles doing there with Silly Creatures?"

"No, Wembley," Red said, shaking her head. "Distress is a thing. It means Fraggles in trouble." Red turned to Mokey. "That *is* a good idea, Mokey. You always have great advice for us when we're in trouble."

"Thank you, Red," Mokey said, flattered. "I would like to help Fraggles in distress. I'll put a notice up on the Big Rock." Mokey picked up her crayon again and took a fresh piece of paper.

TO ALL FRAGGLES IN DISTRESS, she wrote. I WILL SOLVE ANY PROBLEM, NO MATTER HOW BIG OR HOW SMALL. WRITE TO ME, MOKEY, CARE OF THE BIG STONE HEAP TO THE RIGHT OF THE ROUND MOUND.

"How about an adventure story?" Gobo suggested. "I always like reading about something exciting."

"I could do that!" Wembley cried. "I could, I could!"

"It might be a good idea if you wrote that one yourself, Gobo," Red suggested. "After all, as an explorer, you've had some pretty interesting things happen to you."

"That's true," Gobo said. "Or maybe I could write something about my Uncle Traveling Matt. His adventures in Outer Space are *really* exciting."

"Okay," Red said. "Sorry, Wembley. But it does seem right for Gobo to do that one."

"That's okay, Red," Wembley said. "I absolutely agree. Adventure is Gobo's middle name!"

"How about Boober?" Mokey said. "We wouldn't want him to feel left out. What can he do?"

"Boober could write some predictions," Gobo suggested. "Uncle Matt says that newspapers always have a place where someone tries to predict the future. And since Boober is always so worried about what's going to happen, it would be perfect for him."

"Sounds good to me," Red said. "And I'll write something really terrific about...the Volunteer Fire Department!"

"Hey, I'm the siren of the Fire Department!" Wembley squeaked. But it was a very little squeak, and Red didn't hear him.

Red stood up. "Okay, guys," she said. "Time to start the game! Everybody go write your stories." Red looked around for the nearest Doozers. "We'll all meet here in the Great Hall in five Doozer towers!"

Doozers, who also live in Fraggle Rock, are about six inches tall. Doozers *love* to build, and what they build are Doozer constructions. There are Doozer constructions all over Fraggle Rock.

Luckily, the Fraggles love to eat these constructions. To a Fraggle, they taste delicious. And that is fine with the Doozers. There is an old Doozer saying that goes, "When a Fraggle eats a tower, we'll replace it in an hour." If the Fraggles didn't keep eating, soon there would be no more room for the Doozers to build, and they'd have to leave the Rock.

At any rate, one way of telling Fraggle time is by watching the Doozer's build their towers. When a Fraggle sees some Doozers starting on a new construction site, he might say, "I'll be back in a Doozer tower!" This means he'll return by the time those Doozers finish building one of their constructions.

Doozers build pretty quickly, though, and five Doozer towers isn't a lot of time. So Red, Gobo, and Mokey hurried off to start their assignments, leaving poor Wembley standing there with nothing to do at all!

2
The Right-Hand Fraggle

WEMBLEY looked around in dismay.

"Red, wait!" Wembley cried, running after her. "Red! What about me?"

"What about you *what*, Wembley?" Red asked impatiently. Once she started something, she liked to get on with it.

"I don't have anything to do for the newspaper!" said Wembley. "I want to play, too! I'll do anything! Anything at all! Just tell me what!" Wembley hopped from one foot to the other, his tail twitching with excitement.

Red stopped short and looked at Wembley. She frowned. Then she thought hard. What *could* Wembley do? He wasn't very good at anything in particular. He had so much trouble making up his mind that he never seemed to finish anything he started. But Red also knew that it wasn't fair for them to play if Wembley didn't.

Red thought and thought, and then she had an idea. "I know, Wembley!" she said. "You can be my right hand!"

"Gee, that's great, Red," Wembley said, looking slightly puzzled. "But you already have a right hand, don't you?"

"No, Wembley, not my *real* right hand. I mean you can be my Chief Assistant. My Right-Hand Fraggle."

"Wow!" said Wembley. "It sounds really important! Is it?"

"It's only the most important job of all," Red said. "You have to collect all the stories and bring them to me. After all, what if everyone wrote a story but no one handed anything in? There wouldn't be a newspaper at all!"

"What an honor," Wembley breathed. "Right-Handed Fraggle!" He took Red's hand and shook it up and down. "Thank you, Red. Thank you! I won't let you down! I'll be the best Right-Handed Fraggle anyone has ever seen!"

"That's Right-*Hand* Fraggle, Wembley. And you don't have to thank me. This Newspaper Game is fun! Now, don't forget. You have to make sure to bring me everyone's stories before the deadline."

"DEADLINE! GREAT!" Wembley shouted. "What's a deadline?"

"A deadline is a time limit," Red explained. "It tells you when something has to be done."

"Oh," Wembley said. "Like when it's time for me to wake up. That's the deadline for sleep to stop."

"Sort of," Red nodded.

"Or if I was exploring a cave with Gobo and had to be back in time to practice my fire siren, that would be a deadline. Right, Red?"

"That's the idea," Red told him. "The deadline for the First-

Ever Fraggle Rock Newspaper is five Doozer towers from now. Uh, four and a half. Those little guys are really going at it."

Wembley looked over at the Doozer site. The Doozers had already started on the third floor of their first construction.

"A deadline is not such a scary thing," Wembley told Red bravely. "I am looking forward to it." And Wembley sat right down on the ground to watch the Doozers build.

"Aren't you forgetting something?" Red reminded him.

"Am I?"

"The stories," she said.

"Yipes!" Wembley cried. He jumped up.

Wembley had a lot to do before deadline. He had to get all those stories!

He squared his shoulders, took a deep breath, and then stopped short. *Which* story? Whose story should he bring to Red? Where should he go first?

Poor Wembley! He *did* have trouble making up his mind!

Wembley stood there for a long time, trying to figure out what to do. He stood there for so long that he started to get a little sleepy. So he decided to go inside and take a nap.

Wembley slept in a hole that was scooped out of the wall. It

was right above Gobo's hole in the wall. Wembley was halfway to his bed when he noticed Gobo sitting at the table, looking over a stack of postcards.

"Gobo!" All of a sudden Wembley wasn't sleepy anymore. "Hey, Gobo! Guess what? Guess what Red gave me to do on the Newspaper Game? I bet you'll never guess in a million, trillion Fraggle Moons!"

"Okay, Wembley," said Gobo, looking up. "Tell me."

"Don't you want to guess at all?" Wembley asked, a little disappointed.

"I'm busy collecting information for my story on Uncle Traveling Matt," Gobo said. "I don't have much time for guessing games."

"Oh. That's great! Because my job is to be Right-Hand Fraggle to Red, and to collect all the stories for the newspaper! Isn't that terrific? Red says it's the most important job of all! Is your story almost ready, Gobo? Can I see it? When can I bring it to Red? Huh, Gobo?"

Gobo scratched his furry head. "Well, you can see what I've written so far, Wembley. But remember, it's only the beginning. Traveling Matt has had so many adventures that I don't know which ones to tell about first."

Gobo picked up a sheet of paper and gave it to Wembley to read. This is what it said:

Uncle Traveling Matt: Fraggle Without Fear

My Uncle Traveling Matt is one of the bravest of all the Fraggles. Right now he is traveling alone through dangerous Outer Space. He sends me postcards about the Silly Creatures out there and about all the odd and exciting things that happen to him.

"Wow, Gobo, that's wonderful! I'll bring it to Red right away!" Wembley turned and began to run out of the cave with Gobo's story.

"Hey, Wembley, wait a minute!" Gobo grabbed his friend by the tail. "I told you, it's not finished yet! I have to write about all of Uncle Matt's adventures, and how I go into Outer Space to get the postcards, and all sorts of other things, too! There's lots more to tell!"

"You're right, Gobo." Wembley handed the paper back to Gobo. "Maybe the story should be a little longer. Although short stories are nice, too. You can read them faster. On the other hand—"

"Right, Wembley." Gobo smiled. "In the meantime, I have to go see if there's a new postcard from Uncle Matt waiting for me so I can put it in my story. Want to come along?"

"Sure!" Wembley said.

Wembley and Gobo went down a path that twisted and turned. They went through a cave or two and then down a long, dark tunnel.

"When we get back, Gobo, maybe I can help you with your story. Okay?" Wembley tripped over a wompus root.

"Great, Wembley!" Gobo said, picking his friend up.

But by the time Gobo got the postcard and read it to Wembley, and by the time they went back through the tunnel and the cave and down the path that led back to the heart of Fraggle Rock ... and ate some radishes for lunch ... and swam in the Fraggle pool ... and sang some songs ... well, by then Wembley and Gobo were so tired they just had to take a nap.

Wembley snuggled into his bed with a smile on his face. When he woke up, he was going to get Gobo's story, and Red's, and Mokey's, and Boober's. It was going to be so much fun to finish the newspaper!

Wembley fell asleep smiling. Being a Right-Hand Fraggle was the best thing in all of Fraggle Rock!

3
Complications

"WEMBLEY! Wembley!"

Wembley woke up with a start. Someone was yelling his name. Someone was shaking his arm. What was going on?

"Wembley! Right-Hand Fraggle!"

It was Red! And then Wembley remembered. The newspaper! Wembley opened his eyes and tumbled out of bed.

Red was standing there, looking a little grim. "It's already two and a half Doozer towers, Wembley, and I don't have a single story yet," she said severely.

"I'm sorry, Red!" Wembley gasped. "I'll get right on it." Wembley looked to the left, and he looked to the right. Finally he looked at Red again. "Where should I go first, Red?" he said humbly.

Red sighed. "Why don't you try Boober?" she suggested. "I saw him a tower ago and told him about his assignment. He said he'd go think about it."

"Great! Thanks, Red!" And Wembley sprinted out of his cave toward Boober's depressing little hole. He was going to do a stupendous job! Red would have Boober's story in no time!

When he got to Boober's cave, Wembley knocked on the wall and waited. Boober hated Fraggles barging in on him.

Finally Boober's cap, followed by his nose, peered around the doorway. "Yes?" he said. "Oh, Wembley, it's you. Has something terrible happened?"

"No, Boober," Wembley reassured him. "I just wanted to know when your predictions story for the newspaper would be finished."

"Oh. Well, my prediction," Boober said, retreating into his cave, "is that I'm going to forget about predictions and finish my laundry."

Wembley followed him inside. Boober had gathered socks from every corner of his hole and was flinging them into a washtub on the floor.

"But I have to take your story to Red." Wembley was worried. "Do you think it will take you a long time?"

"Probably," Boober said. "And by then Red won't want it anymore, and I will have done all that work for nothing. I'd be better off if I never started it at all."

"Oh, no!" Wembley cried. He could almost see the Doozers busily building their towers. "Red would never forgive me!"

"Well, actually," Boober said grudgingly, "when Red told me I had to play this silly game, I sat down and wrote a little something. Here." He bent over and handed Wembley a crumpled piece of paper that he had hidden in one of his socks.

Wembley uncrumped the paper, smoothed it out, and read what Boober had written.

Boober's Predictions

Today the caves will be damp.

Tomorrow the caves will be damp, and if you stand around in them for too long, you'll probably get a cold.

The day after tomorrow the caves will still be damp, and if you have a cold it could turn into measles. And you'll have splotchy things all over your face and you won't want anyone to see you.

The day after the day after tomorrow, if you still have splotches, you won't want to leave your cave, and soon no one will even remember your name.

The day after that, you'll be so bored and lonely, you'll crawl into a dark hole and stay there, which I wouldn't mind doing, because except for the fact that socks dry faster in the light, I much prefer dark and gloom, where no one bothers me by singing too loudly or laughing too much or having too much fun.

The day after the day after that

The story stopped there.

"Where's the rest?" Wembley asked. "I have to bring it to Red before deadline."

"DEADLINE!" Boober shouted. "Where is it? Did I step on it?" He looked down in horror. "I didn't mean to kill it. Are you sure it's dead?"

"No, Boober," Wembley explained. "A deadline is the time I have to get the stories to Red before. That is, Red has to have the stories before the deadline. I mean—"

"Oh." Boober let out a relieved sigh. "So long as there isn't something—deceased in here." He put his story down on a low rock.

"Listen, Wembley," he said, "before I even think about any more predictions, I have to get my laundry done. You just wait here while I go get some bleach. And don't touch anything." Boober walked toward the door. "I hate it when someone messes with my laundry."

"I won't touch anything," Wembly promised.

Wembley was standing there, waiting for Boober and not touching anything, when he heard a sound. It was a dripping kind of sound. He looked around. Water was dripping from a bucket down into Boober's washtub.

Wembley felt something on his big toe. It was something wet. He looked down. A soap bubble popped and some water dripped on his foot. The washtub was very full of water, soap, and dirty socks.

I wish Boober would get back already, thought Wembley.

He stood there a few moments longer. Then he noticed that his feet felt wet. He looked down again. The washtub had over-flowed and a puddle was forming on the floor.

I should stop the water, Wembley thought, worried. *But Boober made me promise not to touch anything.*

The water was slowly rising. And as he watched in dismay, the paper with Boober's predictions on it floated off the low rock and drifted gently toward the door.

"Oh no!" cried Wembley. "The story!" He grabbed for the piece of paper as it floated past him. It was soaking wet.

Just then Boober came in.

"A flood!" he yelled. "A flood in my home!"

"But I didn't touch anything!" Wembley said anxiously. "Just like you said."

"This is a disaster," moaned Boober. "It will take me longer than forever to clean this up."

"What about your story?" Wembley held out the tiny, soggy mass of paper.

"WHO CARES ABOUT THAT?" Boober yelled. "My floor is wet! My laundry is wet! My life is ruined!"

Wembley quietly backed out of Boober's cave. "Uh, well, I'll see you later, Boober. Okay? Maybe you'll be able to write the story for me then."

But all he heard as he lost sight of Boober was a long, low wail and a steady sloshing sound.

4
It's Later Than You Think

WEMBLEY was in trouble. Time was running out, and he still hadn't brought one story to Red! He hurried away from Boober's hole and down the tunnel toward the Great Hall. He wasn't sure what to do next.

He had almost reached the Hall when his heart gave a great leap. There was Mokey sitting on a ledge with hundreds of pieces of paper around her. Mokey must have finished her advice story! Maybe she had even drawn some pictures for the newspaper! Wembley trotted happily over to her.

Mokey looked up at him, her face full of concern. "Oh, Wembley," she cried, "look at all these letters from unfortunate

27

Fraggles. There are so many of them! I never realized that they all needed my help!" Mokey was getting a strange look in her eye. "It is my duty," she continued, "to try to do something for all these poor, unhappy ones."

"That's great!" Wembley said excitedly. "But do you have your advice story ready yet? I have to bring it to Red!"

"Ah, little Wembley," Mokey said, sighing, "I can't think about something as silly as a newspaper right now. These Fraggles need me." And as Wembley watched in dismay, Mokey gathered up all the letters on the ledge and stood up. "I must go see every one of them and offer my help. Red will understand!" And then she was gone.

Wembley's hands were clammy. He felt terrible for all those poor Fraggles, too, but he felt worse for himself. If Mokey didn't have anything for him to bring to Red, who else was there?

He took a deep breath. Maybe Gobo had finished with his story by now. Surely Gobo wouldn't let him down! Wembley headed over to his cave to find his friend.

Wembley was almost there when he ran smack into Gobo, who was headed in the same direction. "Gobo!" he cried in relief. "I was just looking for you. How is your story? Where is your story?"

"That's what I was coming to tell you about, Wembley," Gobo said. "I was out exploring the caves where the Rock Monsters live."

Wembley had never seen a Rock Monster. But he had heard about them. They were big, scary beasts who lived deep in the far reaches of Fraggle Rock.

"I had my story in my pocket," Gobo went on. "But when I heard the noise, I tripped and it fell out."

"What noise?"

"And then," Gobo went on, "when I turned and saw it, I got scared."

"Saw what?"

"So I threw it at it," Gobo finished.

"Threw what at what?" Wembley was lost.

"Threw my story at the Rock Monster. He chewed it up. Here." Gobo reached into his pocket.

As Wembley held out his hands, Gobo poured hundreds of tiny bits of paper into them. "I'm sorry it got torn into pieces," he said. "But every word I wrote is right there."

Wembley smiled weakly. "I guess I can put it back together somehow. At least," he added thankfully, "the Rock Monster didn't eat *you!*"

"Thanks, Wembley." And Gobo headed off to do something dangerous and brave.

Wembley looked down at the bits of paper in his hands. He knew he could never put the story back together again. He opened his hands in despair and watched the bits of paper drift down to the ground. It was beginning to look like he wouldn't deliver *anything* to Red before the deadline!

And somehow it was all his fault. It wasn't Gobo's fault—Gobo had tried, but the Rock Monster had gotten in the way. It wasn't Boober's fault—his story had *floated* away. And it certainly wasn't Mokey's fault. She was so good and kind, she just *had* to help those Fraggles in dis— in dis— in trouble.

But Wembley had a job to do, and he wasn't doing it. With a sinking heart, he headed off in the direction of Red's cave. He would have to tell her what was happening.

When Wembley got to the Great Hall, the first thing he saw was the Doozers. Four of their towers were already completed, and they were busy at work on the fifth. *Oh, dear,* Wembley thought. *I am a little hungry. And it would be nice to have a little snack. And I could take a Doozer stick off that fifth tower... which would make the deadline come a little bit later....* Wembley reached out his hand toward the tower to pull off a Doozer stick. But he couldn't do it. Slowing down the deadline would be cheating. And whatever happened, a Fraggle *never* cheated at games.

Wembley gulped. Just at that moment Red walked by.

"Uh...Red?" he croaked.

"Wembley! What's up? I haven't seen you around. I was just going for a swim. Wanna come?"

"Red...um...about the newspaper?" Wembley whispered.

"The what?" Red asked.

"The newspaper," Wembley choked.

POOL

GREAT HALL

"The who? Oh, the *newspaper*! I see the deadline's almost here!" Red patted Wembley on the shoulder. "I haven't had a chance to do that story on the Fire Department yet, but I'll get to it. See you!" And Red jumped into the pond.

Wembley just stood there in disbelief. He was a *terrible* Right-Hand Fraggle. He couldn't even bring *Red's* story to Red. Boy, was he making a mess of things!

Wembley slowly turned around. He scrunched his eyes tight shut. He couldn't look. But the Doozers kept building.

Slowly he opened his eyes a tiny bit so that a crack of light showed through. He put his hands up to his face and peeked through his fingers.

The fifth Doozer tower was half finished.

And as he watched, the Doozer construction team hoisted another Doozer stick in place.

Oh, no, Wembley thought.

He was Red's Right-Hand Fraggle, and he was supposed to bring her the stories for the newspaper. He had promised. Besides that, he wanted to show everyone that he could do an important job really well. Nobody really thought he could.

And it was beginning to look as if they were right.

5
Wembley Comes Through

A mean, nagging sort of voice was singing a little song in Wembley's head. The song went something like this:

> I failed, I failed, I failed.
> I don't know what to do.
> I never can decide.
> I want to run and hide.

There was almost no time left. The newspaper deadline was almost here. And Wembley had ruined the whole thing. Red had depended on him to bring the stories in on time, and he had failed. He was lower than the lowest wonkworm. He was a worthless Fraggle.

There was only one thing left to do. He would go back to his cave and find his best of all best friends—Gobo. Gobo was always good in an emergency. He would tell Wembley what to do.

Wembley flew back to his cave. All around him, Fraggles were busy. Some were busy swimming, and some were busy running races. Some were busy playing Roll the Radish down the Hole. Some were busy singing and dancing.

Wembley barely noticed. He tore into his cave, yelling, "GOBO! GOBO!" And then he stopped short. Gobo was nowhere to be seen.

Wembley looked around in despair. And it was then that he noticed the big note that Gobo had left on the desk. "Dear Wemb," it read. "Gone to check for a postcard. Be back in half a tower. Your friend, Gobo."

Wembley sat down at the desk. This was it. He had failed. Red and the others had depended on him, and as usual, he hadn't come through. He never could do anything right.

As he sat there, he idly picked up one of Gobo's crayons and started to doodle on a piece of paper. And then, simply because there was nothing else to do, he began to write.

"The situation is hopeless," he told himself. "But I can at least make some notes. I'll just write down how each of the stories could be written. That way at least I'll have *something* to give to Red when the deadline comes."

Wembley's crayon flew over the paper.

He wrote about Gobo and the Rock Monster. He wrote about all the strange adventures of Traveling Matt, and how brave Gobo was when he picked up Matt's postcards from Outer Space.

He wrote happy predictions for Boober's column. Then he

wrote some gloomy ones, too, because that's what Boober would have written. He wrote advice on how to take the knots out of Fraggle fur, and how to whistle through two fingers, and what to do when you were cornered by a Five-Tongued Thrall so you wouldn't be talked to death. Mokey would have been pleased with the advice he gave.

He wrote about the Volunteer Fire Department, and how exciting it was to be the siren. He wrote a list of events for Red's next Swimathon, and explained the rules of the competition. He wrote about what to wear when exploring strange caves, and how to pack a picnic lunch. He wrote and wrote and wrote, and when he could write no more, he began to draw. He drew pictures of the strange things Traveling Matt described in his postcards. He drew pictures of his five friends.

When he had drawn pictures of all those things and more, he began to write again. This time he wrote puzzles and jokes and riddles:

> Why did the Fraggle knit three socks?
> *Because he had grown a foot.*
> What goes ha, ha, ha, kerplunk?
> *A Fraggle laughing his head off.*

When Wembley was finished, he could hardly lift his *own* head. He could barely move his hand. He gathered all his stories and pictures together and picked them up. They seemed terribly heavy. He could barely stand up. He could hardly see. His head was spinning. He was exhausted.

There was just enough time to bring all of the stories and

pictures to Red before the last Doozer put the last stick onto the fifth Doozer tower. It was all that he could do.

He left his cave and stumbled toward the Great Hall. He walked as fast as he could, which wasn't very fast because he was so tired. The five Doozer towers were in sight now. So were Gobo and Boober and Mokey and Red. In fact hundreds of other Fraggles were there, too, waiting. Watching.

The last Doozer stick was placed on the fifth Doozer tower. The Doozers stepped back to admire their handiwork.

Then every Fraggle there yelled at once. "DEADLINE!"

Wembley tripped and fell. Papers spilled over the ground. Red began picking them up.

"Stories!" she said. "Advice, adventures, predictions. Look at all this. 'Rock Monster Eats Paper,' 'How I Fight Fires,' 'Advice for Fraggles in Distress.' "

"It's a whole newspaper!" Gobo exclaimed.

"It is?" Wembley said weakly.

"It sure is," Red said calmly. "The First-Ever Fraggle Rock Newspaper is finished. It's the very first time I have ever made one, and it wasn't so hard after all."

"Come and get it! The First-Ever Fraggle Rock Newspaper is here!"

Fraggles gathered around, rushing to read all of the wonderful stories. A roar of praise filled the air. "Great job!" "Fantastic!" "Stupendous!" "Fabulous!"

"It was nothing," Red said modestly. "And of course I had a little help from my friends."

Wembley's head was spinning. He felt like there was moss in

his ears. He felt like there was moss over his eyes. He felt like there was moss in his mouth. Something was terribly wrong. He wanted to say something, but he was so tired, he could barely move his lips. "Hey," he croaked, "what about—"

"Terrific Traveling Matt story, Gobo," said Red, patting him

on the back. "I knew you were the Fraggle for the job. And Mokey, this advice is great. I always wanted to know how to take radish stains out of sweaters. And Boober! You even have some *positive* predictions here. That's amazing! Boy, I sure know how to do a newspaper, don't I?"

Gobo's brows drew together in a puzzled frown. "It *is* a great story, Red," he said. "But I didn't write it. My story got eaten by the Rock Monster."

"That's why I—" Wembley whispered.

"And I was so busy I never had time to write my advice story," said Mokey. "I don't understand where this came from."

"It came from—" Wembley gasped, his voice slightly louder.

"And I would *never* write a positive prediction," Boober said. "Positive thinking can bring bad luck. Although this isn't half bad."

"*I* wrote positive—" Wembley stammered. His voice was getting louder still.

"So who wrote all these stories?" Red demanded, looking at each of them in turn. She hardly noticed Wembley, who was staggering to his feet.

"I DID! I DID! I WROTE ALL THE STORIES! IT WAS ME, WEMBLEY! NO ONE EVER THINKS I CAN DO ANYTHING, BUT I CAN!" Wembley's voice was so loud that he startled himself. He opened his eyes wide, hiccuped, and sat down again with a thud.

"*You* did?" Wembley's four best friends gathered around him and looked down in amazement.

"Yes," Wembley said. "Everyone tried really hard to write their stories, but things got all fouled up. And I *had* to hand them in before the deadline. I had promised. So I wrote them all myself. And drew the pictures, too," he added.

"Wow, that's incredible, Wembley!" Gobo exclaimed. "I'm really proud of you."

"Yeah, Wembley," Red added, "I'm impressed. You made a

decision, and you carried through." Red took Wembley's hand and shook it solemnly.

Wembley had never been so happy in all his life.

"I have an idea!" Mokey said. "Let's have a big party to celebrate Wembley's newspaper! I'll make some decorations."

"I'll go get my gourd guitar," said Gobo.

"I'll make sure everyone comes," said Mokey.

"I guess I could bring the food," said Boober. "Maybe I'll make some Radish Delight. Although everyone will probably hate it."

A party might be fun, Wembley thought to himself. "A party could be a good idea," he said quietly. "A party is the best idea I've ever heard!" he cried out loud.

Mokey skipped by, clutching streamers and balloons and party decorations.

Red ran by, yelling "Party!" to whomever she saw.

Boober trudged by with radishes and other good things spilling out of his arms.

Wembley just sat there, so tired he couldn't move. But he wasn't too tired to smile.

Gobo came back, carrying his guitar and a set of Fraggle flutes.

"Hey, what are you going to do for the party, Wembley?" Gobo asked.

Wembley blinked. "Gee, I don't know, Gobo. What do you think I should do?"

There was a long, long moment of silence. Then Gobo reached down and patted Wembley on the arm. "Why don't you just sit there and rest, Wembley," he said. "Just sit there."

And so Wembley sat there while all around him Fraggles

laughed and played and celebrated the First-Ever Fraggle Rock Newspaper. He sat there through Gobo's Sing-Along, and through the Radish Relays. He sat there through the diving exhibition and through the swimming races. He sat and listened and watched and grinned. He couldn't wait to join in. And as soon as he decided just what to do first, he would probably have the best time he had ever had in his whole life!